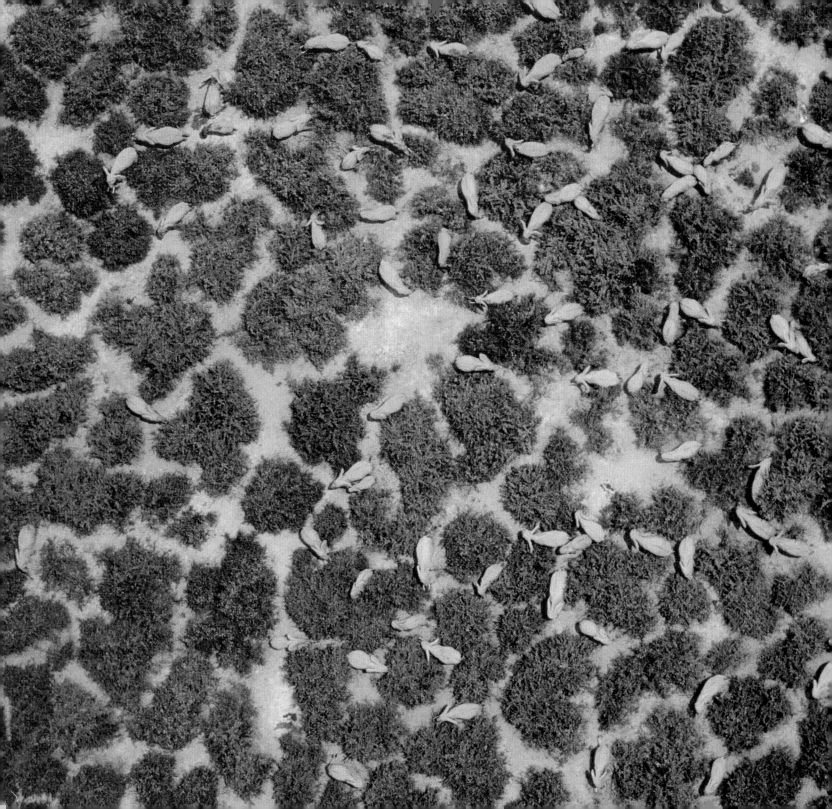

To my children, Saba-Star and Mara-Moon, and all the little elephants.
Oria Douglas-Hamilton

Originally published in the United States, Canada, Great Britain, Australia, and New Zealand by Picture Book Studio,
Ltd. Reissued in paperback in 1996 by North-South Books, an imprint of Nord-Süd Verlag AG.
Distributed in the United States by North-South Books Inc., New York.

Library of Congress Cataloging in Publication Data
Douglas-Hamilton, Oria
The elephant family book / Oria Douglas-Hamilton.
(Animal family books)
Summary: Follows a herd of elephants through the round of its daily and seasonal activities and
explores the relationship between this large animal and humanity.
1. Elephants-Juvenile literature [1. Elephants.]
I. Title. II. Series
QL737.P98D685 1996
599.6'1 - dc20   LC: 95-20725
ISBN 1-55858-549-4 (paperback)

10 9 8 7 6 5 4 3 2

For more information about Oria Douglas-Hamilton and her work, please contact: Friends of Conservation
(elephants), Sloane Square House, Holbein Place, London SW 1 W8NS. Telephone: 171-730-7904

Ask your bookseller for these other North-South Animal Family Books:
THE CROCODILE FAMILY BOOK by Mark Deeble and Victoria Stone
THE GRIZZLY BEAR FAMILY BOOK by Michio Hoshino
THE LION FAMILY BOOK by Angelika Hofer and Gunter Ziesler
THE PENGUIN FAMILY BOOK by Lauritz Somme and Sybille Kalas
THE DESERT FOX FAMILY BOOK by Hans Gerold Laukel

The Elephant
Family Book

Oria Douglas-Hamilton

A Michael Neugebauer Book
North-South Books / New York / London

Far away in Africa there is a beautiful lake, rimmed with a silver crust of salt and sand. Yellow-beaked pelicans and long-legged pink flamingos flock on the shore where elephants and zebras graze.

It is the Lake Manyara National Park in Tanzania. Behind the lake stands a steep mountainous wall known as the Rift Valley Escarpment. Crystal streams flow down through an emerald carpet of plants that look like miniature palm trees. Tall, grey-limbed trees race each other to the sun. Baboons and monkeys jump through the branches, swishing the leaves and calling to each other with chuckles and barks.

I live in a little house tucked under the steep Rift wall with my husband, Iain, and my daughters, Saba-Star and Mara-Moon. It is the research camp and our bush home. Iain built it with stones taken from the Ndala River.
He is a scientist and he studies elephants.

Mhoja is a Park ranger who lives with us and looks after the elephants. Each day we spend many hours with the elephants, taking notes and photographs. We are able to recognize them by the different patterns around their ears.
Iain found out that elephants live in small families a bit like ours.

In the mornings, while my husband and I do our work, the elephant families walk up the river to drink next to the little pool where the children splash and play among the warm rocks. They are not afraid of elephants. Living with elephants in the park has taught them not to make too much noise and to take great care where they play, because elephants are wild animals.

I like best to walk through the forest along the wide elephant paths. They are covered with leaves, rotten twigs, and elephant dung—a soft mat that is the work of the hundreds of cracked, thick-soled elephant feet that have wandered silently up and down these trails for years.

Sweet flowers and the strong smell of elephants mingle and blow in the wind. It is cool and peaceful.

The other end of the Park, known as Endabash, is hot and dry with thick thorny bushes and black tsetse flies, whose bites feel like burning needles pricking your skin. The middle section of the Park is where the flat-topped *acacia tortilis*, or umbrella trees, grow. This is where Iain can climb trees and watch elephants without disturbing them.

At first all elephants looked alike, but after a while we learned to recognize them by the shape of their ears and tusks. They also have different faces and different characters, just like people. Iain first names the biggest elephants after Greek goddesses or well-known women. Then we give names to their children.

Every family has its leader. She is usually the oldest or the biggest member and is called a matriarch. Jezebel, Curie, and Hera are matriarchs and live in the Park together with the five hundred other elephants.

Curie is easily recognizable with her single straight tusk, which makes her look as if she is holding a giant knitting needle in the side of her mouth. Tusks are long teeth and are made of ivory. Curie's tusk is a perfect tool to jab any elephant that gets in the way, or chisel into the side of trees and strip off bits of juicy bark, which she loves to eat. Curie has a daughter called Pili who is four months old.

Hera has curved tusks of different shapes. She is also known as Mama Kali, which means "Fierce Mama" in Kiswahili (the language the people speak in the land of the elephants).

Hera used to charge our car as we drove through the Park, but now she is calmer. She has an eleven-year-old daughter, Yusta, named after Mhoja's own daughter.

Mary is an old matriarch who leads another family, and she has the most beautiful tusks of all the elephants in the Park. She is easy to recognize, with the big cut in her right ear. Elephant ears are shaped like the map of Africa.

One day in August something special happened in Curie's family. Two little elephants peered out at the world for the first time. They have just been born. They are twins; the first twins to be born in the wild to a known family of elephants. Everyone was happy to hear that twins had been born, for they are rare in elephant families. We call their mother Bahati, which means "Luck" in Kiswahili. They are her first babies and have spent 22 months in her womb.

With two new little baby boys in the family, there is much confusion, and Bahati moves from one to the other. She gently lifts one to his feet, holding him against her leg until he can stand. The other one is hungry. He sucks his little trunk as if it is a thumb, but he does not yet know how to use it.

All the elephants, big and small, come to look at them.
With outstretched trunks they touch and smell them. They are only a few hours old and are covered in soft hair. Newborn babies weigh about two hundred and fifty pounds (one hundred kilos) and stand three feet (one meter) tall. Babies must learn to walk as soon as possible, for there are many predators around.

We notice that the twins are smaller than most other newborn elephants. Their little ears stick out like fans, and their toenails, five on each forefoot and four on each hindfoot, look as if they have been scrubbed clean.

One twin is taller and the other is fatter. The shorter one has to stand on the tops of his toes to feed. He fastens his little pink mouth to the teat, sucking and gurgling and gulping. His tail hangs to the ground like a little bottle brush.

As soon as the twins are strong enough to walk, Bahati leaves the place of their birth and heads down to the river. Curie and Hera walk ahead and younger cousin Yusta follows nearby.

We discover that one twin has a bend in his tail and other has a straight tail, so we name them after their tails.
This is the true story of Crooked Tail and Straight Tail.

Young teenage sisters and cousins like Yusta are the nannies or baby-sitters, and are very important for the survival of the baby elephants. Caring for the families' babies prepares Yusta to become a good mother.

While Bahati and Hera are looking after the twins, Yusta stands protectively next to Pili to be sure that she does not wander far from the family.
Unlike our families, elephant brothers and male cousins leave in their teens and join the fathers, grandpas, and uncles, who live on their own and visit the family only occasionally.

Like all male calves Crooked Tail and Straight Tail have to suck frequently to get enough milk, and drink about four gallons (fifteen liters) a day. Little male calves grow faster than females, and are always hungry. But now the twins will have to do with less milk, as they are two, and Bahati, as a new mother, has breasts that are not yet fully developed. Babies like to touch their mothers with their little trunks while feeding.

Elephant mothers usually have a baby every four years and can supply milk all their lives. Some babies will suckle up to six or even eight years if their mothers allow them.

Even though the twins were born with teeth, two on the top jaws and two on the bottom jaws, shaped like the soles of little gym shoes, they cannot eat solids until they are about six months old. An elephant will have six sets of teeth in its life.

The African elephant's trunk is a nose, and a hose, and an arm tipped with a two-fingered hand—all in one. Equipped with thousands of muscles, the trunk can pluck a tiny leaf from a branch six feet (two meters) above the head or pick up one seed at a time from the ground. The trunk is also used to lift a heavy log, pull down a branch, or even carry a baby. It can clean eyelashes or scratch inside the ear by using the two fingertips, and it can be cupped like a hand to collect sand when digging a hole.

The trunk is the survival tool of the elephant. It is the elephants who use their trunks to dig the water holes in times of drought, and all the other mammals, birds, and insects come to drink as well. When resting, the trunk can be folded up between the tusks.

The trunk can also detect smells far or near, and is used to talk to other elephants. Elephants have many different ways of communicating with each other—loud trumpets, little growls and rumbles, and even sounds so low that we cannot hear them. By using a special part of their trunk and throat, they can send out secret sounds called rumble calls that travel long distances and can be picked up by the big elephant ears.

By midday Bahati reaches the pool at the Ndala River. Like all elephant babies of their age, Crooked Tail and Straight Tail can drink water only with their mouths. They are so thirsty that they walk into the water up to their eyes, with only the tops of their backs visible. Straight Tail seems more organized.

He keeps the tip of his trunk out so that he can breathe and drink at the same time. Crooked Tail, however, sticks his trunk onto the bottom of the riverbed, holding his breath. A big bubble bursts between his eyes, and he has to fling his trunk up, breathe, and start all over again. After drinking, they scramble onto the warm sand and collapse among the rocks.

Silently, Curie leads the rest of the family farther downriver, where the water flows gently over the sand, and they step into the shallow water, cooling their feet. One by one, they drop their trunks and suck up as much water as their trunks can hold, which is about a bucketful.

Then, lifting their trunks, they spray the water into the back of their mouths, which sounds just as if they were filling up cans with a garden hose.

It is now time for the elephants to move to a nearby mud wallow and stand around it as if it were a bathtub, collecting mud in their trunks and slapping it to the left and right of their bodies, over and under their heads, as if they were doing their exercises. Pili slides into the mud bath and rolls over. She loves playing in the mud.

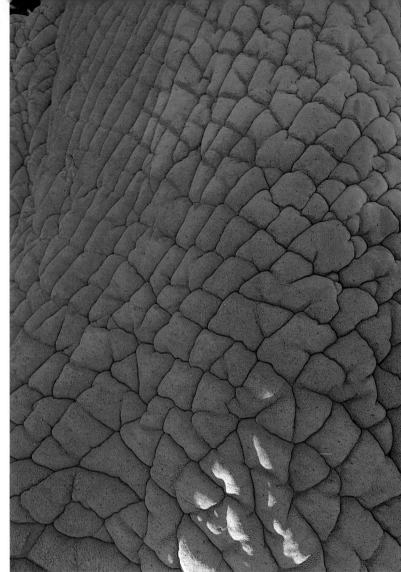

After drinking and washing, it is now time for grooming. The elephant is covered with a thick layer of skin, which is a loose latticework of wrinkles that looks a bit like mud that has dried and cracked. To keep their skin cool and cleaned of parasites, elephants cover themselves with gooey mud, just like chocolate sauce. Mud is very important to elephants.

By using the sharp ends of their toenails, Curie, Hera, and Bahati dig out some earth, which they collect in the tips of their trunks and then blow behind their ears and around their necks like talcum powder. Then they move to a special tree, where they rub and scratch their mud- and dust-covered skin. It feels so good. When all the family has completed their grooming, they settle under a big shady tree to rest. The babies flop onto the soft, cool ground, and surrounded by a grove of legs and trunks, they fall asleep.

When Pili and the twins wake up, they feel hungry. Since they are less than one year old, they can easily walk under the elephants like bridges. The twins follow Pili.

When they reach Hera, who is old and grouchy, she watches Straight Tail from the corner of her eye and kicks him with her hind leg. This sends him sprawling onto his chin, which makes him squeal. Bahati and Yusta run over to help.

Each pulls a twin between her two front legs, where he is safe. The twins immediately try to suckle, but Yusta has no milk.

Even though Crooked Tail is smaller, he always pushes ahead of Straight Tail, establishing his position right behind his mother. The twins always suck together. Crooked Tail prefers to feed on the right side of his mother and usually gets there first.

Bahati, like all mother elephants, has two breasts behind her forelegs.

By the end of the second month the twins are more playful. Their favourite game is to climb over each other.
Pili, who is slightly older but much stronger, chases the twins. They catch on to each other's tails and wind their trunks into knots.

One day when Mhoja is on patrol in the woods below the Rift, he hears elephants trumpeting and the sound of breaking branches. Curie suddenly comes crashing past him with her family close behind. She stops to listen. Her ears stretch out and up like huge fans, her head is held high, and her trunk is lifted up like an arm to catch any sniff. Mhoja notices that Hera is wounded and blood is pouring out onto her side. Yusta puts earth on her wound, pinching it together with the tips of her trunk as if they were fingers. Curie, sensing danger, quickly moves on and without slowing her pace heads toward Endabash and the spiky bush.

Mhoja runs up the hill through the woods and suddenly spots two men armed with spears running as fast as they can through the bushes. He chases them, but they get away. They are poachers, coming into the Park to kill elephants for ivory. They are not allowed to hunt in the Park, for this is a special place where wild animals can live without being hunted or trapped.

We are very worried, especially for the twins. Curie keeps the family hidden for a whole month and returns to the flat-topped umbrella trees when Hera's wound is completely healed. The twins are very thin. Curie has to spend all day in search of food and wanders farther and farther away.

Bahati is unable to keep up with her and stays alone near the water and shade.

One day we find Bahati on the lake shore with a young bull. We look through our pictures of all the elephant faces and discover that he is Bahati's cousin Taurus, who has not been seen since he left the family at the age of thirteen. He may have heard Bahati's secret rumbles and come to her when she was alone calling for her family. We are happy that she has someone to help her guard her two sons.

We are in the middle of a drought. Now five months old, the twins try to chew at bits of wood and shrubs, stumbling behind Bahati like two little blobs. Bahati does not have enough milk to feed her two hungry boys. Crooked Tail and Straight Tail are much thinner, resting often in the shade under their mother. Straight Tail is weak, his little face pinched, and his skin all dry. Just two weeks before the seasonal rains come, he dies.

It is very sad that we will never see Straight Tail again, but with an extra portion of milk, Crooked Tail survives.

Then big black clouds arrive and thunder echoes down the valley. Even the sky looks as if it is crying. The rivers and the mud wallows fill up. The elephants return and Crooked Tail and Pili roll in the mud, blowing bubbles and chasing each other. Crooked Tail pulls at the new grass with the little fingers on the end of his trunk and stuffs the grass into his mouth.

Some months later we spot all the family, and there is a nice surprise that cheers us up. There are two new babies walking next to Hera and Yusta. Both are boys. We name Hera's son Liziki, and Mhoja names Yusta's son Marang, after the great green forest that spreads across the top of the Park. By now Crooked Tail is so fat, we can hardly recognize him.

Curie has disappeared, perhaps having died of disease, which leaves Pili once again in the care of Bahati and Yusta. Pili in turn helps guard the little babies as their new nanny. Hera takes over the leadership. Now that she is a mother and matriarch, she displays her old habit of threat charges, keeping her name Mama Kali. And so the family responsibility passes from one matriarch to the next.

The grass grows like never before, in a thick, beautiful garden of golden flowers. It is soft and smells so good. Everyone can hide and play games in it. While we follow the elephants, Mhoja takes care of the children, mine and the elephants', too.

Elephants are our biggest land mammals. They have been in Africa for a very long time, much longer than humans have. In fact, as far back as 6 million years ago, the elephants' ancestors—known as primelephas—roamed right across the middle of Africa.

A fully grown male elephant stands as tall as two doors—over thirteen feet (four meters)—and is twice the size of a fully grown female elephant. He weighs up to eight tons (six thousand kilos), which is the same as ten big oxen, and he can eat 400 pounds (150 kilos) of food a day. If he ate only apples, that would be about nine hundred apples, but instead the elephant eats all sorts of leaves, seeds, branches, vines, and grass. Eating keeps him very busy.

It will take about thirty years for Crooked Tail to be fully grown. He will wander over great distances and meet up with other elephants. He will use his tusks and his growing strength to fight other males.

His head will be wide, and he may live sixty-five years and grow a pair of tusks that weigh 130 pounds (50 kilos) each. But these days very few big males roam the African bush, for most of them have been shot by poachers or hunters for their ivory.

Between 1980 and 1990 more than 650,000 elephants were killed, mostly illegally. Their tusks were sent across Africa and to countries like Japan, Hong Kong, and China and then sent to the United States of America and Europe as carvings and trinkets.

The tusks were cut up into small pieces and made into boxes and bracelets, statues and chopsticks, letter openers, and many other items. Some of the bigger tusks were carved and polished, and everything was sold as ivory. But since the worldwide ivory trade ban in 1990, no tusks or trinkets have been sold legally.

When an elephant dies, other elephants come to carry away the bones and
tusks. This is the strange and wonderful way that elephants bury their dead.
We hope that elephants can live in peace now, so long as the ivory ban lasts.

Because elephants are so big and live for so many years, they need much space to live in. Africa still has space, and the elephant belongs to Africa.
But as long as people buy ivory, other people will kill elephants. You and I need to teach people not to buy ivory. We must be sure that no one will want to kill our friend Crooked Tail. If we help, then one day he may have his own little baby elephant on the plains of Africa with a crooked tail just like his.

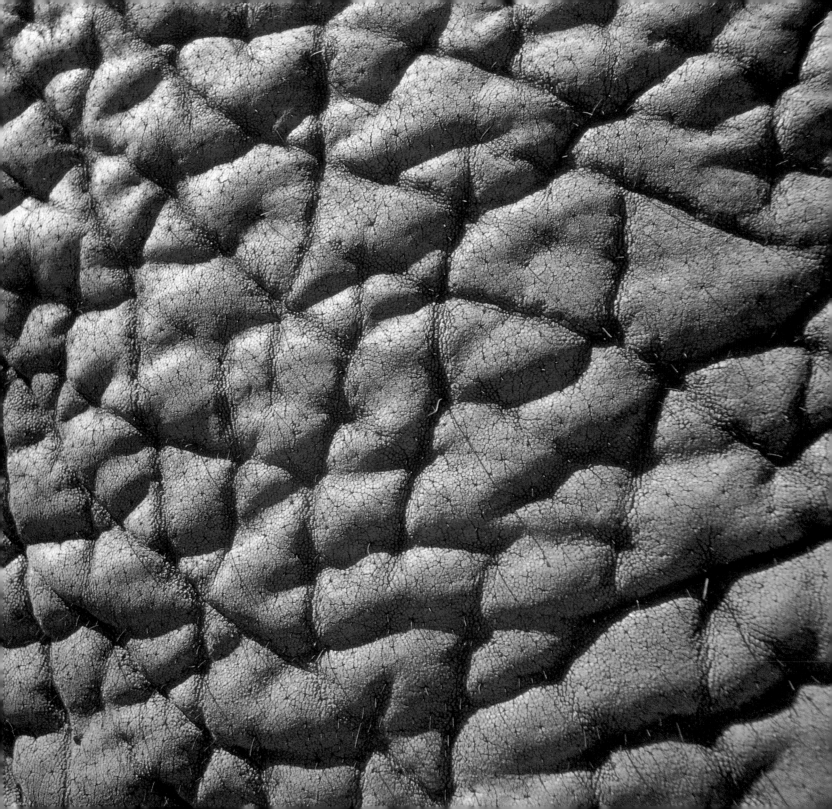